Laughter Lines

Also by Des O'Connor

BANANAS CAN'T FLY: THE AUTOBIOGRAPHY

LAUGHTER LINES

Comic Verse for Life's Little Moments

DES O'CONNOR

SIDGWICK & JACKSON

First published 2014 by Sidgwick & Jackson
an imprint of Pan Macmillan, a division of Macmillan Publishers Limited
Pan Macmillan, 20 New Wharf Road, London N1 9RR
Basingstoke and Oxford
Associated companies throughout the world
www.panmacmillan.com

ISBN 978-0-283-07218-5

1 3 5 7 9 8 6 4 2

A CIP catalogue record for this book is available from the British Library.

Printed and bound by CPI Group (UK) Ltd, Croydon, CR0 4YY

For Jodie, Adam, T.J.,
Samantha, Karen and Kristina

Contents

INTRODUCTION

If you were to ask me why I've started writing poems, I would say, well, there's a simple answer. I don't think I *am* writing poems. Yes, some of the lines in my verses rhyme but I honestly wouldn't call myself a poet. I like to think of my offerings more as 'comic verse'.

Recently my young son Adam, who is nine, came home from school and said, 'Dad, listen to this:

I wish I was a glow-worm
I never would be glum
'Cos how could I be miserable
When the sun shines out my bum?'

Hardly Keats or Wordsworth, but it made me smile. Then I realized that Adam was aware of my own attempts at comic verse, and this was his way of telling me that he approved. But it also reminded me of a comic poem I'd heard many years before, which impressed me so much that I filed it away in my head. I believe it was written by the marvellous comedian Robb Wilton. Here's what I remember of it:

A sail on the sea is the thing that suits me
And I've done some sailing, it's true.
One night at Land's End I was at my wits' end
On a night when I'd had one or two.
The Captain came out on the bridge and he said,
'Lads, we are doomed. The old tub's going down.
To the boats, every man – except you!'
I said, 'Me?' He said, 'Yes! There's no room: you must drown.'
I said, 'Drown?' He said, 'Drown.
The old tub's going down, don't stand arguing there.
I've just told you straight, there's no room for you, mate,
In the boats – or in fact anywhere.
I know it's upsetting but what's the use fretting?
We might have lost all of the crew.
But now as I say we can all get away
And only lose one – and that's you!'

It still makes me smile – the taste of absurdity and the rhythm and rhyme within the piece inspired me even back then to think that one day I might write something with similar ingredients.

Most of us have at some time or other found ourselves caught up in situations that ruffle our feathers and to which we react instantly – but not always with the best results. Experience has taught me that if we are able to see the funny side of any problem then that problem becomes much less of a concern.

Humour can help to put the mildly annoying incidents of life into true perspective – it certainly helps when dealing with life's little stress tests.

Let me give you an example. About ten years ago I was invited to spend a day with friends at the Royal Ascot race meeting. I was excited and looking forward to the occasion, and hired myself a smart grey morning suit and top hat. When the morning came, it took about an hour to get ready. A final check in the mirror confirmed that I'd chosen the right outfit; even if I say so myself, I looked quite good, and I found myself smiling as I left the house. Earlier that morning heavy showers had threatened to put a dampener on the day, but now the clouds and rain had surrendered to the sun. It felt good just to be alive.

Then I did something I will never understand. Something I had never done before. When I stepped out directly on to the wet lawn I instantly felt my feet moving away from my body. I saw the lawn hurrying towards my face. The impact as I met the turf, face first, was surprisingly mild. So there was no real damage, no broken bones. But my outfit was now looking a bit sad.

The smart grey morning suit had become a crumpled, mud-splattered, dark shade of khaki, and the once-smart Ascot top hat now resembled a battered old football.

For a few moments I just lay there in silence. Then the initial shock began to fade, followed by a feeling of utter stupidity. How could I have done such an idiotic thing?

Then, as my brain began to return to some kind of normality, I started to giggle. I heard myself saying, 'Well, that's another fine mess you've gotten me into, Stanley' – followed by, 'Are we still going to Ascot?'

Ascot! Looking the way I did? I doubt they would have let me on to the racecourse, let alone into a private box. I smiled at the mental picture of a mud-drenched Des bouncing in and wishing everyone a happy, enjoyable day. I went back inside the house, had a bath and then watched the races on TV.

But the foolish and unexpected experience of that morning taught me a very valuable lesson. Sure, I had ruined a good suit and I had missed out on a special day, but that's all. Nothing life-threatening, tragic or traumatic had happened.

So what did I learn? Well, for starters, don't get upset over things that don't really matter. Don't let life's little problems become big problems. Recognize the ironic, smile at the silly side of life. If one day you find yourself smartly dressed and lying face down in the mud, try laughing at yourself.

And I hope as you read what follows you'll find something that makes you smile, something that will help you recognize how to play the funny cards that life sometimes deals us.

Have fun laughing at life!

DES

1

The World's Best Dad

I am the proud father of four wonderful daughters. Happily we are all very close and I adore them. But dads can become a little too protective of their daughters, especially during their teenage years . . .

Hampson

Teenage Fashions

Have you ever said to your daughter,
Are you really going out in that?
You look like an advert for Oxfam
Or something dragged in by the cat.

Well think of the stuff we used to buy
And the gear we wanted to wear:
Teddyboy suits, crêpe-soled shoes,
Flares and Mohican hair.

It's the same with teenage girls today.
They want to be fashion queens
Dressed in flimsy low-cut gowns
They've seen in magazines.

Brand new jeans with holes in,
Perfume you smell down the street,
Handbags bigger than dustbins
And high heels that ruin their feet.

There's lots of tattoos they order,
They've got them all over the place.
One girl's got one south of the border
And another she'd like to replace.

It's the same with the metal piercings,
That's a thought that gets on my wick.
We used to need charm to pull a girl
Now a magnet will do the trick.

Yes, fashion today seems a bit OTT,
Like stuff on a catwalk show.
Styles have changed and so must we:
Be cool and go with the flow.

Don't worry if outfits are daring
And they go out looking like tramps.
But say no if she ever starts wearing
Just a plaster and a couple of stamps.

Tune in, be a little more 'with it'.
Say she looks 'wicked' and then,
'Have a fun night, just live it.
But make sure you're home by ten.'

Let me tell you a relevant story. I have always been a fan of Perry Como, who recorded some beautiful songs which became worldwide hits. One evening in America I was fortunate to hear Perry sing 'The Father of Girls' on stage. He was a mature senior citizen at the time, but his performance, as always, was sensitive, relaxed and heartfelt. When he finished he told the audience, 'My daughter is a constant source of joy. When she smiles she brightens my every day. The sun shines from an azure sky and my world becomes a happier place . . . Of course, she's sixty-two now!'

Yes, daughters can make you smile, no matter what age they are. When my daughter Samantha was just five years old she was invited to a friend's birthday party. As she left, my wife told her: 'Have fun, but if anyone asks you any questions about Daddy just say, "I don't know".'

When Samantha came back from the party my wife said to her, 'Did they ask anything about Daddy?'

'Yes,' Samantha said, 'they asked me, "Who is your father?".'

'What did you say?'

'I said I don't know!'

As well as my lovely daughters we are blessed with a young son, Adam, who is a joy. So I do know a bit about becoming a dad.

To Be A Dad

So you've just become a father,
Well that bit's easy enough.
But now it's time to diversify
And I warn you it's gonna get tough.

You'll do jobs that you never dreamed of:
A doctor, a chauffeur, a clown.
A male Mary Poppins, a gofer,
A dad on a merry-go-round.

Queuing for hours at Disneyland,
Every theme park's a similar thrill.
They'll expect you to join in the action,
Go on rides that'll make you feel ill.

And wait till you change your first nappy.
You'll hardly believe your luck.
Little boys can do projectile piddling
And you just have to learn how to duck.

Then there's the dreaded sleepover,
When their little friend comes to stay.
They have lots of fun . . . till a quarter past one
And you just can't get up the next day.

The weekends used to be fun days
With that extra hour in bed.
You'd watch the big match on the telly;
Now you'll watch Cartoon Network instead.

But one day a year will be special.
You'll get a card that makes you smile.
It's from your lass or lad to 'The World's Best Dad',
And somehow it's all worthwhile.

A Kid's Birthday Party

My little lad's just had a birthday
So my wife threw a do for our son.
I've been counting the cost of that party
And I'm telling you now it's not fun.

When I was a kid all my mum ever did
To celebrate my special day
Was give me a card and a bag of sweets
And let a mate come round to play.

But nowadays, that's not enough.
It's like an Olympic event.
All the mothers compete with each other;
They book a clown or a big white tent.

A bouncy castle to 'keep the kids moving',
Party poppers and lots of balloons.
If they just want to keep the kids moving
Why not give 'em a big bowl of prunes?

There's at least thirty kids at each party.
They run round the house like hell.
They eat like a swarm of locusts
And their mothers need feeding as well.

The kids eat whatever's on offer:
Cupcakes, jam tarts and more;
They come back for repeats like ice cream and sweets
And one always throws up on the floor.

And there has to be a theme for each party:
Spiderman or pirates or such.
I suggested 'The Garden of Eden' –
Well, the costumes wouldn't cost much.

Now each kid has to have a goodie bag,
If they don't get one, they complain.
Every bag costs more than a fiver –
That's when you say, 'Never again!'

But I know I don't really mean that.
I love the boy, and I'm glad that he's mine.
But maybe we can change his birthday –
To February . . . 29!

It's Snow Joke

I don't mind when it rains, I can put up with fog,
I don't care if the wind starts to blow.
But there's one bit of weather I really dislike:
That's the four-letter word called 'snow'.

I know it looks nice on a Christmas card
It makes you want to say 'Ahhh'.
But it can stop all the trains and ground lots of planes
And sometimes you can't start the car.

When there's snow on the ground and the 'flu going round
With its cold cures, powders and pills,
The energy firms are not bothered
All they do is put up your bills.

And we've got a neighbour who's proud of his garden
'It looks better than yours,' is his claim.
But when it snows through the night and everything's white –
Well, ours looks exactly the same.

Yet snow just excites my youngster.
He says it's fun, and the boy is no fool,
Well he knows if it snows and none of it goes
They'll probably be closing the school.

Then it's time for the dreaded toboggan
And there's a snowman that has to be built.
(It must be worse if you're living in Scotland
And the wind starts to blow up your kilt.)

So I guess I should learn to put up with snow
If my son and his friends think it's fun,
But on cold winter days I'd much rather laze
On a warm sunny beach in the sun!

2

King of the Road

Most men love their cars and I am no exception. But I have to admit I have never been a fan of Formula One racing. I am probably in the minority but I just don't find Grand Prix events exciting. So here are my thoughts on some possible improvements.

The Madness Of Formula One

I've always been a keen sportsman.
I can sit and watch sport every day.
Any sport on TV you could mention –
With the exception of one, I must say.

I love football, tennis and cricket,
Sumo wrestlers who weigh half a ton,
But you'll never catch me buying a ticket
For the madness of Formula One.

I don't understand why they do it,
All that driving at breakneck speed.
They go round like hell and you never can tell
Which one is the one in the lead.

The whole thing's bizarre, what's the point of a car
That goes as fast as it does?
You wouldn't survive on the M25,
You'd be nabbed and grabbed by the fuzz.

As a sport on TV it's just boring.
So if they want to get more viewers back
Make it much more of a challenge:
Put some cyclists on the track.

Let's have traffic lights and diversions,
Potholes and bumps on the road,
A couple of school bus excursions,
And a lorry that's shed all its load.

Mark some of the road 'No Entry'.
Put out millions and millions of cones.
Leave holes unrepaired for a century
And let drivers start using their phones.

Let's have a few level crossings,
The police and the fire brigade,
Roundabouts and a bus lane
And some horse guards on parade.

And the best test of all for the drivers?
See who drives with patience and care
When stuck behind a slow-moving caravan
On the road to who knows where.

I enjoy driving but I am a little apprehensive and reluctant when it comes to stopping and asking for directions. It may sound like a simple enough task but it rarely is. First there's the slight hesitation as they maybe recognize me.

'Hey, you're 'im off the telly, aren't you? What's your name? Don't tell me! What are you doing round here?'

Suddenly I'm involved in their lives, their families. 'My mum loves you!' they say.

They seem to completely forget that I'm asking directions, and don't notice if I'm holding up the traffic. I'm very fortunate in that I seem to live in a world of no strangers, and I usually enjoy meeting folks but it can become a little awkward if you're lost. So a satnav is the answer. Unless, of course, it goes wrong.

Something's Gone Wrong With My Satnav

Something's gone wrong with my satnav.
I can't rely on it now.
Last week it took me to Birmingham
Via Croydon, Chiswick and Slough.
And I really loved that satnav:
No worry, no panic, no stress.
I could drive in peace and in comfort
As it took me to each new address.

So while on vacation I bought a replacement
From a bargain shop in Korea.
It had an Aussie bird giving directions,
Like, 'Just chuck a U-ey here.'
The old one had a posh lady –
My friend, a guiding light.
I just loved the way that she used to say
'Your destination's ahead on the right.'

Now we're back to struggling with road maps
And stopping to ask the way
Not that my hubby would ever do that –
'I know where we are,' he will say.
Then we'll finally arrive at twelve forty-five
(That's twelve forty-five in the morning),

When the party is over, the guests have all left –
And yes, that's another day dawning.

So I've got to get *another* new satnav
No matter what the cost,
For me it's a definite must-have
And my hubby can go and get lost.

TURN
RIGHT

The Traffic Cop

The traffic cop signalled the car to stop,
It was moving a bit erratic.
'Blow into this,' said the traffic cop.
'I can't,' said the man, 'I'm asthmatic.'

'Then we have to take a blood sample.
I smell booze upon your breath.'
'I can't give blood, I'm a haemophiliac.
If I did I could bleed to death.'

'Well I think that you've been drinking,
A urine test will check the amount.'
'I'm a diabetic so I can't do that either,
It could lower my blood-sugar count.'

'Right, get out of the car and walk this line.
I've had enough of all your junk.'
'I'm sorry officer, but I can't do that.
And that's because . . . I'm drunk!'

3

A Popular Show on the Telly

I'm often asked if I'm Irish. I usually reply, 'Well, I'm of Irish descent . . . My granny fell down the stairs in Belfast!'

In actual fact, my father's mother was Jewish and she married an Irishman from Cork. Their wedding announcement was not exactly welcomed by either family but the bride and groom were in love and that was all that mattered. And anyway, a mix of chutzpah and blarney was not such a bad recipe for my father to inherit.

My mother's father was Welsh and her mother's line included Dutch and German ancestors. So I guess I can be described as a Heinz Variety! (But I still support England when the World Cup comes round.)

Who Do You Think You Are?

There's a popular show on the telly
Where they trace back your family tree,
They do it with the help of computers
But it looked pretty easy to me.
So I did some DIY genealogy
But I must have got part of it wrong
'Cos according to me I'm a hundred and three
And my granny's alive in Hong Kong.

Then I checked on the computer, I was eager to know,
Did I come from pedigree stock?
But what I found was quite disappointing,
In fact it came as a bit of a shock.
It seems most of our lot were scoundrels.
Though one was a dandy, for sure –
He had nine illegitimate children,
And a seizure while trying for more.

Yes, there's been some black sheep in our family
And none of them made me feel proud.
One hanged for treason (we don't know the reason,
It's all been kept under a cloud).
One 'Jack the lad' went to prison,
Somehow he fell foul of the law.

You could say in a way he was like Robin Hood
Except he stole from the rich . . . *and* the poor.

But one of our line worked for royalty:
Henry the Eighth, no less!
He advised the king on accountancy
Or whenever Henry was stressed.
The best advice he ever gave him
Was when a divorce was near.
He said, 'Just forget about alimony,
I've got a much better idea.'

Now I've had it with DIY genealogy.
I'll let my family's past be
And in a hundred years, or maybe more,
They can waste their time checking on me.

A, B or C?

I was watching *This Morning* this morning
And a commercial break was due.
I was yawning and having a cuppa
And wondering what next I should do.
Then the lady said, 'You can win £10,000,
Just get on the phone now and dial!'
As I wrote down the telephone number
I couldn't resist a smile.
Well I spend a lot of time on the Internet
And the question was easy for me:
What comes after 'B' in the alphabet,
Is it 'A', is it 'B' . . . is it 'C'?
How I wanted to shout – I had no doubt –
So I reached out and picked up the phone.
And I got it right! The answer was 'C'.
But it seems I wasn't alone:
Apparently hundreds of thousands rang,
And everyone thought it was 'C'.
So somebody else got the ten thousand quid,
And the call cost me 95p.

Fifteen Minutes Of Fame

I've seen a lot of people on TV
Who really can't sing or dance
But if we all get fifteen minutes of fame
Then maybe I still stand a chance.
It's not that I'm a musician.
I'd be no good at reading the news.
I can't cook, or do things in the garden,
So which TV show should I choose?

I don't fancy *Strictly Come Dancing*;
Rehearsing for weeks could be hell.
If I did the splits I could damage some bits
And I might pull a muscle as well.
I wouldn't last a week in the jungle –
I don't fancy a Bushtucker Trial,
I couldn't eat kangaroos' privates –
And I won't go on *Jeremy Kyle.*

The show I most like is *Mastermind.*
It's intelligence there that's the key.
But you must have a specialist subject
And the only one I know is me.
I might try out for *Eggheads,*
But you can't do that show on your own.

For *Millionaire* I'd be there if they asked me,
Except I don't know a friend I could phone.

I could have done well on *The Price is Right,*
Take the Money or *Open the Box.*
Sale of the Century? Maybe *Bullseye*?
Or the Palladium's old *Beat the Clock*?
Strike it Rich, or *Play Your Cards Right,*
Blankety Blank or *Winner Takes All* –
So many shows I'd have been on,
But somehow I never did call.

Maybe my time has passed now
And my chance, sad to say, has been missed.
A few moments of fame and that instant acclaim –
It's a shame. Yet I've still got the list!
But you know, I don't really regret it.
Who needs fifteen minutes of fame?
I think I'll just be a critic,
And let someone else take the blame.

Hampson

4

Everyone Needs a Good Holiday

All entertainers have to travel. Well, you have to do the show in peoples' home towns – the audience won't come to your house! Travelling has changed a lot in recent years, especially air travel. There are so many security checks to get through, and taking off your shoes and removing your belt in public can be a bit embarrassing. There are other hazards too.

When I am invited to appear on stage or television abroad, it's very nice if the organizers offer to fly me first class or send a limo to pick me up at the airport, but it's not something I insist upon. In fact, one of my most memorable travelling experiences came after I had to fly at short notice with one of the no frills, cut-price airlines.

I was on holiday in Spain and had to fly to Leeds to complete some programmes for Countdown. *Now I didn't really mind sitting for a couple of hours with my knees up around my ears. And I had to smile when it was announced that there would be a sale of the ham and cheese baguettes – honestly! Apparently all sandwiches would be reduced to just £1 a time. But the return flight is one I won't forget for other reasons. About twenty-five minutes before we were due at the departure gate at least twenty ladies appeared, colourfully dressed in pink shirts, pink cowboy hats and white cowboy boots. Boldly emblazoned in silver diamante on their shirts were the words: 'G-String Gillie's Gang'. All were in high spirits, heading to*

Estepona to celebrate Gillie's hen night. I had slightly mixed feelings when I realized we would all be on the same flight. And when they spotted me, they really let rip.

'Hello, Des, do you wanna be in our gang, our gang ...'

Then they started warbling the Countdown *theme, following it with a non-stop flow of gags. One of the lines must have been referring to the* Countdown *clock: 'Can* you *last thirty seconds, Des?'*

They were very funny and I hope they had a wonderful time on their break. They certainly kept us all entertained!

I've Just Got Back From A Holiday

I've just got back from a holiday.
I think I now need a rest.
It's years since I've been on an airplane
And I must say, I wasn't impressed.
First I had to go through security;
They made me take off my belt and my shoes,
Then a bell went off and they frisked me –
And we hadn't even been introduced.

They've got what they call a full-body scan,
It can see right through your clothes.
It shows all your bumps and your dangly bits
And I'm a bit shy about those.
They took away my nose clippers,
They saw them as a threat I suppose,
Like I might burst in on the captain
And pull all the hairs from his nose.

The departure gate was a heck of a walk,
Lugging booze from the duty-free.
And then we got robbed at the snack bar:
Four quid for one cup of tea!
Once you're inside that's when you're advised
What to do if the plane lands at sea.

The door opens wide, you just jump on a slide
I mean, how much fun can there be?

Your life jacket is under your seat
With a whistle for attracting attention.
But if you're bobbing up and down with sharks all around
That's the last thing I think they should mention.
Then you wait for an age for your luggage;
I helped an old lady get hers.
Her case nearly gave me a hernia,
But the news that they gave me was worse.

My luggage was on its own holiday
To a place that's called Martinique.
All I had was what I stood up in.
I wore the same shorts for a week.
So that's the last time that I go abroad.
No more scary airline trips.
Next year I'm off to sunny Southend
For a beer and some nice fish and chips.

The English Abroad

Everyone needs a good holiday
Away from the work and the stress.
Pack a case, choose a place where the sun shines,
But one thought I'd like to impress.

You can spot new arrivals from England
With their flip-flops, sandals or Crocs,
Long khaki shorts and a golf hat,
And of course their black woolly socks.

They lie on a sunbed all day long,
Cooking in the midday sun,
Like a prawn or a sausage on a barbie,
In a couple of hours they're done.

So if it's ninety degrees in Fahrenheit
Get a book and relax in the shade.
Don't be fooled, it won't be any cooler
If it's thirty or so centigrade.

There's a special suncream for the English.
It protects while you're out and about.
It's simply called Factor 1,000 –
When you squeeze, an umbrella comes out.

So be careful all you Brits abroad
When the holiday's just begun.
Don't be mad dogs and Englishmen:
Stay out of the midday sun.

Hampson

Hotel Goodies

I don't think my wife is dishonest
But when we stay at hotels overnight
She believes when we leave it's OK to thieve
Yet somehow it doesn't feel right.

Cotton wool, shampoo and shower caps,
The biscuits they leave for a snack,
Notepads and biros and hangers,
And anything else she can pack.

It's a wonder we don't get arrested!
One time when we went on a cruise
She got nail files and clippers and warm woolly slippers
Plus a shoehorn that she'll never use.

On that ship she behaved like a looter –
I remember the look on her face.
I think she'd have taken the trouser press
But it just wouldn't fit in her case.

The last time we went up to London
We stayed at a Park Lane hotel.
Then I saw the rate. I didn't feel great.
So we took the curtains as well.

A Coffee Shop In America

I was in a coffee shop in America,
At a posh hotel in LA.
My waitress was new, she hadn't a clue.
Well, she'd only just started that day.

I told her, 'I don't need a menu,
But I'd like a nice up of tea.
Maybe a couple of eggs and some bacon.
That will be fine for me.'

What she did next was amazing.
She rattled off the menu by heart.
'There are so many eggs that we have, sir,
I'll tell you a few for a start.

'We have scrambled eggs, curried eggs, eggs a la Russe,
Freshly squeezed juice on the side.
Eggs over easy, eggs Benedict,
Poached eggs, boiled eggs or fried.'

I said, 'Look, I'll just have some bacon.'
'Yes, sir – honey-cured, grilled or fried?
Hickory, Danish, Canadian?'
I said, 'I'm sorry, I just can't decide.

'Look, I won't bother with bacon,
I'll just make do with some toast.'
She said, 'Yes, sir, it's a pleasure to serve you.
Which toast do you fancy the most?

'We have brown toast, white toast and sesame,
Melba and cinnamon as well.
French toast – well that's best for me.
And you'd love our French fries I can tell.'

I said, 'Look, I don't think I'll bother.
I'm beginning to lose the will.
And I've got to be off to the airport.
So could I just have the bill?'

She said, 'Is that Visa, Diner or Mastercard?
American Express is OK.
Missing you already, sir,
Leave a tip –
And have a nice day!'

5

Magical Days with Mum and Dad

I am a fortunate man. When I think back to my childhood, it's always with a smile. Although my parents struggled to make ends meet at times, they provided a happy and secure home for their children. My dad was a natural comedian who would lighten even difficult moments with a joke.

When I recall the dark early days of the Second World War, I still hold so many happy memories of that time. I was about ten and my sister Pat was eight when we were evacuated away from the nail-biting tension of the London Blitz and I remember how Mum was over the moon when Dad decided to leave his London job to join us in Northampton. It felt so good to have the family together again.

My sister and I loved our visits with Mum and Dad to the cinema. Every Thursday on our way home from the pictures, we would pop in to our local fish and chip shop. And although they served your food wrapped in newspapers, it always tasted delicious – salt and vinegar, crispy chips and white, fresh, flaky fish.

They really were magical days.

The Fleapit

As a child I loved the cinema.
They weren't posh like the ones today.
We called our local 'the fleapit',
It was rough but we went anyway.

Some of the films were scary,
There were scenes that kids shouldn't see,
Like a fight with a mongoose and cobra,
And that was in the seat next to me.

We saw Tarzan swing through trees with Jane,
When beauty and strength combine.
But Tarzan would often yell out with pain
When Jane didn't grab the vine.

My favourite films were the Westerns:
Roy Rogers and Trigger, of course.
In one film he shot all the outlaws
While playing guitar on his horse.

When Indians attacked the wagon train,
The cavalry would save the day;
They'd blow a few notes on a trumpet
And frighten the Apaches away.

And now the old fleapit's no longer around,
But the memories I still recall.
All the laughter and joy I found as a boy,
For just sixpence a night . . . That's all!

Mum And Dad

My dad was a dustman, my mum was a char.
Every cent that Dad had we spent –
And he never had much so it didn't go far.
At times, not as far as the rent.

I wore hand-me-downs each day to school,
Not a pretty sight to see.
Wearing hand-me-downs I felt like a fool
Well, my sister was bigger than me.

We didn't have central heating.
The only heat we had was the sun.
At times Dad would suck on a peppermint
And we'd all sit round his tongue.

If central heating had been suggested
I know what Dad would have said.
'Central 'eating? One tooth in the middle.
That's a very strange way to get fed.'

My mum was a staunch Sagittarius
And every day she would check out her sign.
It once said, 'Your future's precarious',
So she started reading mine.

I was born a Capricorn.
It's the sign of self-esteem.
Well, Jesus was a Capricorn,
And Elvis was one of our team.

Mum said, 'Never marry a Virgo.
It won't work out, I'm afraid.
You'll get up in the night for a piddle,
Come back and the bed will be made.'

These moments to me are so special.
The best times that I ever had.
Magical moments and memories
Of the days with my mum and dad.

Turning Into Dad

I think I'm turning into my father
I'm saying things he that he used to say.
'They don't write songs like they used to,'
And, 'Things were different in my day!'

But Dad always knew how to make me smile
With jokes he'd told me before.
And every time he made me laugh
I'd love him a little bit more.

We once went to see a Frankenstein film
When I was a twelve-year-old tot.
They said, 'The boy looks a bit small for sixteen.'
Dad said, 'Yes, well he worries a lot.'

Dad could always come up with a funny line.
It was wonderful when he did.
Someone once said, 'Are they all your own teeth?'
He said, 'They should be: they cost fifty quid.'

Dad would sometimes forget things.
(As you mature it happens a lot.)
I was about to say what he did last Sunday
But I'm embarrassed to admit, I forgot.

Now I've got my own son and we laugh all the time,
When he smiles it's so good to see.
And if he loves his dad as much as I did mine,
Maybe one day he'll turn into me.

One of my dad's favourite gags is about a man who knocks at the door, saying, 'I've come about your advert for a handyman.'

'Are you a carpenter?' the lady of the house asks him.

'No.'

'An electrician?'

'No.'

'A decorator?'

'No.'

'Well, what makes you think you are handy?'

'I live just round the corner.'

6

Why Do We Fall for the Same Old Guff?

I like to think I'm a people person; I get interested in the highs and lows of their lives. But I have to be honest and admit I am not that thrilled when complete strangers ring me at home trying to sell me something. They always start by asking lots of questions. 'Are you insured?' 'Do you have double-glazing?'

I try to let them know politely that I'm not interested but if they just carry on with their sales pitch I start playing verbal games. I'll ask them ridiculous and silly questions.

'Are you married?' 'Do you have children?' 'Are you going to have any more?' 'Would you like to buy an old pram?'

Then I try to sell them whatever they are selling me, only I make the price much cheaper. They get very confused.

Try it sometime (but disguise your voice). It can be fun!

Cold Calls

I'm not too keen on cold calls.
They always ring when you haven't got time.
Then they start trying to sell you things
And they just won't get off the line.

So I tell them to leave their home number;
I say, 'I'll ring you back in an hour.
Let's hope you're not having your dinner then,
Or just getting into the shower.'

But they won't let you ring them at their place.
Just keep asking. It drives them insane!
Then go read a book, leave the phone off the hook
And they'll never call back again.

We All Went To School

We all learned to add up,
We can all count from one to ten,
So why do we fall for the same old guff
They catch us with time and again?

If a coat was on sale for, say, thirty quid,
And everything else seemed fine,
We might hesitate to pay that thirty quid
But twenty-nine, ninety-nine is fine.

It seems we won't part with a hundred pounds,
We don't want to go quite that high.
But ninety-nine, ninety-nine – that's different.
Well it sounds like a bargain buy.

Have we finally lost all our marbles,
Have we all gone a bit deranged?
Be flash, pay a hundred pounds cash,
But make sure you ask for the change.

Does anyone know why we have to put the clocks back or forward? Who came up with that idea? I forgot to put the clocks forward once and when the alarm went off in the morning a panic started. We were all running around, one hour late, in a world of mayhem and madness. It's not the best way to start your day. Leave the clocks alone I say!

The Clocks Go Back

The clocks go back on Sunday.
So we get another hour in bed.
But what sounded at first like a good idea
Has become the time that I dread.

Why do we have to change at all?
Why get up when it's not even light?
The clock's playing tricks, it's seven, not six
And somehow it doesn't seem right.

What's the point of putting the clocks back?
Who decides this crazy rule?
The buses all leave at unusual times
And it's hard getting kids off to school.

They say 'early to bed and early to rise'
Will help every man make his mark.
They tell us the early bird catches the worm
But who wants to eat worms in the dark?

The same thing happens when you suffer from jet lag.
The time change alters your mood.
You go out for a meal and feel sleepy;
You go to bed and you just want some food.

My friend owns an antique clock shop
With two hundred clocks on the wall.
When his alarm goes off in the morning
Lots of cuckoos are making the call.

And it's not only cuckoos that wake him up,
There are bells and chimes as well.
It sounds like the world is sending
A cacophonous medley from hell.

But the worst time of all in his clock shop,
When from cursing it's hard to refrain,
Is at two a.m. in the morning
When they're changing the clocks once again.

Hampson

Politicians

Not everyone likes politicians,
It's not often they keep their word.
'Vote for me and you'll see new conditions' –
That's a promise that everyone's heard.

MPs always seem to make headlines,
Front page, centre stage in the news.
Some come out of the closet or lose their deposit
But there's more than that they can lose.

They are losing the trust of the public,
And maybe the common touch.
And the folks who were always supportive
May now vote for Screaming Lord Sutch.

MPs have fiddled expenses.
The amounts they tried to claim!
They've been charged with driving offences
And then let the wife take the blame.

But they'll be there for the paparazzi.
Well, kissing a baby looks cute.
They'll put on a big smile and pose for a while
Till the baby throws up on their suit.

Politicians are like babies' nappies
And politicians don't always excel.
They should be changed as often as possible
And for the same reason as well.

7

Mysteries

Sometimes in our lives we are confronted with little mysteries. Why is it so hard to get the label off a non-stick frying pan? Why don't birds fall out of trees when they sleep? Why can't we tickle ourselves? Often we stumble across the answers but now and again, well the world just doesn't seem to make sense.

Hampson

Rubbish

Why do we worry about rubbish?
Why can't we dump it all in the bin?
Plastic bottles and jam jars and eggshells
And whatever else I want to put in.

Leftovers from yesterday's dinner,
Fish bones – 'long time no sea',
Flowers now past their sell-by,
It's all much the same to me.

Now the bins are all different colours.
If you don't sort things right you get fined.
Each one goes out on a particular day.
Get it wrong and they leave it behind.

You can't today just throw stuff away
The way that we all used to do.
Don't know where the disposable nappies should go?
The colour might give you a clue.

And now they're using a camera,
Installed in your bin, if you please.
They get snaps of last night's supper –
Spaghetti balls covered in cheese.

It's up to us to live with the pong
While paying our increasing rates.
I'm beginning to lose the will to live
And I'm losing some of my mates.

When the dustman calls this Christmas
I'll say, 'OK, the Council win.
I've put your tip in a bin this morning.
But I can't remember which bin it's in.

'I know all these rules may not be your fault,
You're just doing what they tell you to do.
But my problem is, I'm quite colour-blind –
So traffic lights are a problem too.'

Still, I'll do what the Council are asking,
Even though it's a bit of a cheek,
If they'll empty our bins like they used to:
Which was, of course, once a week.

The Nosy Neighbour

I've got a new neighbour who's just arrived.
She's nosy, and a bit of a snob.
There's a big flashy car parked in her drive
So I reckon she's got a few bob.

She cycles every day to aerobics
On a bike that she keeps in her yard,
Wearing dangly earrings, bright pink trainers,
White tights and a red leotard.

At nine every morning she's out jogging.
She's dead keen to keep weight off her hips.
She's had Botox, fillers and facelifts,
And she's done something weird to her lips.

Now you may say that it's me being nosy.
How rude! I'm not nosy at all.
But something odd is going on in her garden –
Don't know what, 'cos she's built this big wall.

And I damaged my ankle on Friday,
You might say I was being too keen.
I was trying to see what she's up to
When I fell off my new trampoline.

I'm just trying to be a good neighbour
And do things that good neighbours do.
So I've bought a new video camera
And I've got some binoculars too.

No, I don't like folks who are nosy.
Mind your own business, I say.
Just concentrate on your own life
And let everyone go their own way.

The Health Shop

There's a health shop at the top of our high street.
It hasn't been open that long.
It sells stuff which I've never heard of
And some of it smells a bit strong.
Everything they sell is organic of course
But let me give you my grandma's advice:
Organic doesn't make any difference at all
But you can bet it will push up the price.

They sell strange-sounding breakfast cereals,
Food that they call 'new age';
Muesli that looks like what you might find
At the bottom of a budgerigar's cage.
They sell bread that doesn't even taste like bread
Or anything else I recall.
No wheat, no flour, no salt, no yeast –
It tastes like nothing at all!

They sell garlic and kelp and sesame seeds
And some chocolate that helps you get slim
And odd-looking packets of seaweed
That make you feel good when you swim.
They also sell something called hemp oil;
It comes in a little brown jar.

They say it will help you move faster –
I might get some of that for the car.

They sell hummus, tahini and baba ganoush
And mung beans from Singapore
And something I dread called sourdough bread
That looks like it's been on the floor.
There's some stuff they sell in flour bags,
I haven't a clue what it's for.
But if there's ever a flood, you could keep out the mud:
By sticking it under the door!

They've got pills for gout and verrucas
And face cream they say keeps you young.
Rice milk and soya and wheatgrass
And a repellent so you don't get stung.
Well I got stung at that health shop:
I went pale when I saw the bill.
And they've just hung a sign in the window:
'We are closed . . . 'cos the owner is ill!'

8

Age is Just a Number

I'm a firm believer in the saying 'age is just a number', as you'll see in this chapter. I've never understood why people fib about their age and spend years insisting they are nowhere near collecting their pensions, then later in life they can't wait to boast, 'Next year I'll be ninety!'

I've also never really understood why people try to take years off their age by plastic surgery. The hilarious Joan Rivers famously joked about going under the knife. I remember her telling me how difficult it could be for a comedienne to retain her femininity and yet still be able to make an audience roar with laughter. Joan admired the way Lucille Ball always managed to look glamorous on screen even in the goofiest of television sketches. I think she would have smiled at 'Cosmetic Surgery Sale'.

Cosmetic Surgery Sale

We're all so concerned with our image,
It's something we like to discuss.
Well, a new cut-price surgery has opened –
They call themselves 'Tux R Us'.

Everyone likes a good bargain
And an offer they can't resist.
Tux R Us have now got a sale on,
So outside they've put up a list.

Amazing things are on offer.
They'll put collagen in your veins.
You can get Mick Jagger's lips for a fiver –
And use them to unblock your drains.

But most of the deals are a rip-off.
They just stretch things, or move bits around.
You can get a bum-lift for a tenner –
They promise it won't touch the ground.

One lady had silicone implants,
With the maximum double-G cup.
Now she has found she looks good lying down
But not so good when she sits up.

They do deals on cellulite dimples,
Discounts on bingo wings,
Ointment in tubes for men with big boobs
(It doesn't do much . . . it just stings).

Nose jobs and Botox and a trout pout
For less than three quid a jab,
Whatever's gone south they can lift up no doubt,
But you have to go home in a cab.

One woman tried liposuction
Then owned up that her funds were slack.
She was short fifty quid. You won't believe what they did:
They drugged her, and put it all back!

To this story of course there's a moral.
Beauty, it's only skin-deep.
So if you don't look so hot and it's all gone to pot,
Well, don't get it fixed on the cheap.

More December Than May

I took a look in the mirror this morning,
I looked more December than May.
But what was the cause? Was it male menopause?
Or was I becoming passé?

I've tried to keep up with fashion,
I once wore a thing called a thong.
I thought I looked 'cool' till it shrunk in the pool.
I try but I get it all wrong.

So today I bought me a onesie,
I was told that's the 'hip' thing to do.
But a onesie's not fun if it won't come undone
When you need to run to the loo.

And I took my first 'selfie' this morning,
Still under my new-onesie spell.
My nose looked like Pinocchio's
And it was out of focus as well.

So fashion, I guess, just isn't for me,
Being 'cool' and 'up to the minute'.
But out of fashion I will never be,
'Cos I was never really in it.

Grandma's Got A Computer

I got an email today from my grandma.
She has taken advice, it appears.
She went out and bought a computer.
Which is brave, considering her years.

But she's finding it all quite confusing,
All the jargon and computer talk.
Someone asked her if she's got a website.
She said, 'No, it's the way that I walk.'

The new words are driving her crazy –
Download, megabyte and mouse.
When they told her a mouse was required,
She put traps up all over the house.

Now she's not keen on YouTube and Twitter,
And Facebook's not her cup of tea.
'Well it don't sound desirous to pick up a virus
That ruins your whole PC.'

She's been told that her PC can freeze up,
Stop her surfing and browsing and such.
She thinks it's too late to be Googled
A thought that's not thrilling her much.

So tomorrow she's selling it all on eBay.
She thinks the whole thing is a risk.
You can view everything that's on offer:
Her broadband and two floppy discs.

She's decided it just doesn't suit her.
She'll just hang out her washing 'on line'.
Use the kid next door's computer –
He knows how it works . . . and he's nine!

Birthdays

As ladies mature, or get older,
Not many reveal their age.
Every year they get younger and bolder
And reluctant to turn the page.

My neighbour next door just turned thirty-four.
Well, that's what she said to me.
In fact she just turned the numbers around –
She's actually forty-three.

Ladies start fibbing about their age
When they're young, flirty and sporty.
And the longest five years of a woman's life
Are the years between thirty and forty.

But it's not just the ladies who alter their age.
Men lie, if their engine has stalled.
They say they don't care, then put dye in their hair
And they lie even more when they're bald.

But some men have a renaissance,
Saving their best for the finish.
Some even become fathers again,
So not everything starts to diminish.

There's one man I should mention, who's now on a
pension,
He's seventy-seven at least.
He's got rid of his zimmer and looks a lot trimmer
And he says his libido's increased.

But as you get older I'm told that you shrink.
Well, that can't be true, I must say.
'Cos when I put on my socks every morning
My feet are getting further away.

But age is only a number.
So have a life, have a laugh, have a ball.
Be the life and the soul of the party
And never grow old at all.

The Happy Funeral

Auntie Fay has passed away,
Her funeral is set for next Monday.
She left a message for us all –
Could we try to make it a fun day?

'Please don't wear black. Just wear a smile,
And hold back on the tears.
Think of all the fun we've shared
Through all of these happy years.

'Don't let the day get too gloomy.
I won't be lying in state.
Send the flowers to a hospice
'Cos I'm past my smell-by date.

'Have some fun, tell some jokes,
Say some nice things about me.
Have a drink and eat up the sandwiches
You might as well – after all, they are free.'

Her only concern was her little black cat
Who slept every night by her bed.
'Who's going to hold her and pet her?
And who'll make sure that she's fed?'

Fay said to me once, 'I want to be clear,
You can't be buried with your pet.'
When I asked her why, she simply replied,
'Well, what if it's not dead yet?'

We didn't know that she wasn't well;
Whinging wasn't her style.
And what she left us in her will
Was the memory of her smile.

She did leave her zimmer to the vicar
And the stairlift to her old friend Flo.
But Flo doesn't need a stairlift –
She lives in a bungalow.

So let's try to make Monday a fun day.
No tears, no sadness, no fuss.
And when it's our turn to go, somehow I just know
She'll be waiting by those gates for us.

HAVE FUN!
Hampson

9

Love Through the Ages

I married Jodie in September 2007 at Highclere Castle (which later became the location for the television show Downton Abbey*). We shared a wonderful day with family and friends. Jodie looked stunning but during the exchange of vows she became a little tearful, and as she paused to wipe away her tears our three-year-old son Adam, with perfect timing, called out in a clear voice, 'I love you, Mummy.'*

In that completely unrehearsed moment the entire congregation knew our little boy was speaking from the heart. There was laughter and more than a few misty eyes. Adam had just made our memorable day even more memorable. It was a truly magical moment which we will treasure forever.

I honestly believe that the best recipe for a happy marriage should always include a good sense of humour. So never go to bed on a disagreement.

Stay up all night and fight!

Hampson

Thirty Years Of Marriage

Women don't always say what they mean
When they talk to their other half.
They may sound sincere with 'darling' or 'dear'
But sometimes they're having a laugh.

Men also play at this silly game;
We do what the ladies do.
Why don't we say what we really mean?
Here's an example or two.

We go out shopping together;
She tries on six pairs of jeans.
I say, 'That pair there was perfect,'
But that's not what I really mean.

I'd like to say, 'What a waste of a day,'
But I'm trying to be discreet.
What I really mean is, 'I'm starving,
Let's go and get something to eat.'

Or to say to the wife when she's cleaning,
'You're working too hard, it's a shame.'
I mean, 'Switch off the vacuum cleaner
Then at least I can hear the game.'

When the washing machine won't turn on,
And she asks, 'What's the best thing to do?'
I simply say, 'That's women's work.'
When really I haven't a clue.

But we know each other inside out
And the jokes and the moans apart
She knows that I really do love her.
That's the truth and it comes from the heart.

The Perfect Love Life

Every woman hopes to find
A man who's the love of her life.
The first ever perfect husband
And she'd be the perfect wife.

Well, here is a cast-iron recipe
To satisfy her every desire;
If she's looking for a perfect love life,
These qualities the man will require.

Be a man she can rely on.
A man who's handy round the house.
A man who can always make her smile.
A man who's not a mouse.

A man who would never tell her lies.
A man with a powerful career.
A man who doesn't drink or smoke.
A man who is always sincere.

But this sound advice will only work
If one rule she can always recall:
It is vital that all of these men
Do not know each other at all.

The Wedding

Harry married Annie on Friday,
An unusual sight to see.
For Annie had just turned ninety-six,
And Harry was 103.

Annie always had a crush on Harry.
'We'll get married one day,' he'd say.
But she never believed they would marry.
Until one day Harry's wife passed away.

And on Friday they went on their honeymoon.
Of course they didn't travel too far.
They spent the entire weekend together
Just trying to get out of the car.

My One And Only Blind Date

I've only ever been on one blind date
I was twenty-one at the time.
My best mate talked me into it,
He said the girl was sublime.

So we arranged to meet by the tea bar,
Near the clock on platform two.
I was wearing a red carnation.
(Well, on a blind date that's what you do.)

Like a scene from *Brief Encounter*
I was lost in a romantic dream
Hoping I wouldn't be stood up
Then she appeared like a ghost through the steam.

My pal had said she looked quite exotic,
Typically French, but small.
Not the Brigitte Bardot I remember,
No, she looked more like General De Gaulle.

'Let's go for a bite in the pub now,'
Was the very first thing that she said.
Then she ate non-stop for an hour;
All I saw was the top of her head.

She knocked back a bottle of bubbly
And ordered the tart of the day.
She said that I looked lovely
As she slowly started to sway.

She whispered as she was leaving,
'If I'm late my husband gets grim.
I'd like a large gin for the journey
And a doggy bag for him.'

Now if my pal had said she was married
I'd have run like a bat out of hell.
He never said her old man was a boxer
And they'd got six kids as well.

So it's the only blind date that I've been on.
I don't think it works for me.
It's not something that I could get keen on,
No I'll just stay home alone, fancy-free.

10

Animal Crackers

I once played a vet in a sketch on television. The action took place in my surgery and my first visitor was Rod Hull's way-ward emu.

That emu was a nightmare! It attacked me and I was thrown over a couch. None of it was rehearsed . . . and I won't tell you where it put its beak but I couldn't ride a bike for a week.

Now every vet has my admiration.

The Vet's Waiting Room

I arrived with a headache this morning –
I am the local vet –
I'm afraid that I was yawning,
As everyone brought in their pet.
All of them needing attention,
Looking for help, I presume,
There's a few I really should mention
Out in my waiting room.

There's a crocodile with a toothache,
There's a camel with the hump,
There's a giraffe with tonsillitis,
And a frog who's scared to jump.
There's a Cheshire cat who never smiles,
A pig who's gone off his food;
There's a flock of sheep that can't get to sleep,
And a monkey who's quite rude.

There's a leopard who has changed his spots,
A skunk who smells quite nice,
There's a polar bear with polaroids
From sitting on the ice.
There's a dog who has never had his day,
There's an owl who has never been wise,

There's a bull who they say is a little bit gay,
And a hyena who just cries.

There's koala bears and kangaroos,
Wiggly worms and rats,
A cat that's used up seven lives,
Some crickets, and some bats.
There's a zebra in his pyjamas,
A greyhound who never runs,
A gorilla who hates bananas
And my day has hardly begun.

But always be kind to the animals,
Take good care of your pet.
Pat 'em and pet 'em and show 'em your love
For like the elephant, they'll never forget.

Getting A Dog

All the family went off to the shelter,
To get a dog we could call our own.
We bought a collar, a lead and a name tag;
Some biscuits, a dish and a bone.

There were Great Danes and tiny chihuahuas,
And poodles and spaniels to see.
We oohed and we aahed for hours,
But to choose one we couldn't agree.

I wanted one that would scare an intruder.
'Get a "BEWARE OF THE DOG" sign,' I said.
Then my wife – well, I have to include her –
Said, 'Get "BEWARE OF THE OWNER" instead!'

But she loved all the Scotties and Yorkies,
The way they 'sit' and offer their paw.
And how they wag their tail when it's 'walkies',
The moment you open the door.

When we narrowed the choice to a trio,
Every dog received lots of fuss.
Then a dachshund broke loose from his kennel
And we didn't choose him – he chose us.

He was long but strong with little short legs.
And in winter we very soon found
With his belly so low he just wouldn't go
When there's very deep snow on the ground.

At first we didn't know what to call him
But he's part of the family now.
At home we all just call him 'Snowballs' –
Well, it seems to be right somehow.

I know some people love their pets so much they treat them as family. They spend fortunes on pet insurance, vets' bills, doggy outfits, Christmas and birthday presents.

Some dogs are not only allowed to sit on the couch, they are encouraged to do so. And a few get to sleep on (or even in) their owners' beds. But I was still taken by surprise, when I was in America recently, to see that a rather unusual celebration was about to take place.

The Doggies' Wedding

I have just come back from a wedding,
A wedding of class and style.
The bride wore a perfect white dress,
But the groom, he just wore a smile.

For this was a canine wedding,
He was poor and she was rich,
He was a down-at-heel mongrel
And she was a pedigree bitch.

Yes, the bride and groom were doggies
But real love knows no bounds.
Their tails wagged away on this special day
For two very lovesick hounds.

They'd met by the Pampered Pet Parlour,
He was hungry and didn't look right,
So she'd offered him the rest of her doggy bag
And it was love at very first bite.

The wedding was posh with plenty of nosh,
There were biscuits and goodies galore.
Some guests were dressed in doggy coat vests,
And they offered their paw at the door.

There were Yorkies and poodles and bichons,
Winners of pedigree cups,
And the groom had some friends from Battersea
Who had never even heard of Crufts.

Then, when the service was over
The vicar announced with a deal of pride
'I am happy to say you are married,
And you may now sniff the bride.'

Hymn 200

11

Junk in My Drawers and Other Bad Habits

I do believe it's very important to have a friendly relationship with your doctor. But it is a delicate situation. You can be genuinely pleased to see your doctor at the surgery, but in all honesty you'd rather not be there at all. I'm lucky that my doctor has a finely tuned sense of humour. He likes to laugh – well, laughter is the best medicine – and I get him smiling sometimes with old comedy routines like these:

'Doctor, the invisible man is outside.'
'Tell him I can't see him.'

'Doctor, the seven dwarfs are outside.'
'Tell them I'll see them shortly.'

'Doctor, there's a man outside who says you've stolen his A–Z.'
'Tell him to go and get lost.'

Hypochondriac

I like to sit down with my doctor
And discuss all my fears, man to man.
'Cos I might have something contagious
Or maybe I might need a scan.

I'm there every day in his waiting room
Suffering from who knows just what.
And I sit there and stare at the others
And wonder what illness they've got.

I don't think my doctor much likes me.
He says I'm a bit highly strung.
He spends lots of time with the others,
But just gets me to stick out my tongue.

Last year he asked for a favour.
Would I help clear away all the snow?
At the time he was checking my prostate
And that's not the time to say no.

He keeps telling me I shouldn't worry.
He thinks I'm just swinging the lead.
He says I'm as fit as a fit butcher's dog.
But *my* butcher's dog is dead.

Today I don't feel a hundred per cent.
It could be my general malaise.
Unless I'm a hypochondriac –
Well, that's what my gynaecologist says.

So I think I might change my doctor
And maybe I'll make out a will.
It can't *always* just be 'man 'flu'.
And maybe my doctor is ill?

Why Swear?

I hope that I'm not being silly
Or being a bit of a prude
But why do people swear willy-nilly –
Are they just expressing a mood?

Now and then, well of course I get angry.
But I don't swear when I'm not amused.
It may sound absurd but I say different words,
Not the ones that are usually used.

I say 'yoiks' in moments of anger
And 'sugar' – well, that's not obscene.
I've been known to say 'oh fer-fer-forget it!'
I don't swear, but they know what I mean.

When last week our vicar came round for lunch,
My wife got herself in a flap.
She made him an old-fashioned hotpot
Then dropped the whole lot in his lap.

Well, I've never heard him swear before.
He used words that I won't say now.
Words you don't expect from the vicar
(And I don't mean 'Holy cow').

And never swear in front of the children.
It's not wise, nor the right thing to do.
What's the point of using abusing words
When they probably know more than you.

Clutter

I've just read that clutter can fog up the brain,
And I'm worried 'cos I'm someone who stores
Things I'll never use like worn out old shoes –
There's too much junk in my drawers.

Why do we hang on to useless stuff
Like biros that haven't got ink,
Batteries that have long since run out of puff
And a plug that won't fit any sink?

I've found LPs and singles I can't play any more
(Well my turntable's now obsolete),
There's a pair of odd slippers I never took back
'Cos somehow I lost the receipt.

And that old wicker basket where the cat used to sleep,
Some coins in champagne corks,
The picnic set we bought on the cheap,
With the plastic knives and forks.

I've found a Millennium diary
And a Valentine card from some nut.
Among all the clutter there's a bent rusty putter
And a miniature fridge that won't shut.

A faded picture from my schooldays?
I don't know why I didn't bin it.
It's a Polaroid shot of my first school play
And I wasn't even in it.

Some old garden shears not used in years,
A plant that has long since died –
Why do we keep trash in the garage
And leave a valuable car outside?

Well now I've made my mind up,
It's time to change my ways.
Out with the old and in with the new:
Enter a brand new phase.

I'll get rid of the junk and the rubbish,
The waste of good space is a crime.
I'll start first thing in the morning
Or as soon as I've got the time.

12

Let's Talk Proper Again

What's happening to our language? Why are the meanings of words changing? 'Wicked' isn't wicked anymore, and 'sick' now means 'cool'. It's hard to keep up and easy to get things wrong. Even when you aren't using slang, words can trip you up.

Apparently in the late Forties the Archbishop of Canterbury flew to New York. On stepping off the plane, he was confronted by a posse of American journalists. The very first question they asked was, 'What do you think of all the prostitutes in New York?'

'Are there any prostitutes in New York?' the Archbishop innocently replied.

The next day one of the newspapers reported that the first thing the Archbishop said on arrival was, 'Are there any prostitutes in New York?'

So let's be more careful with what we say and how we say it!

Au Pair

My wife and I made a decision.
'If we both go out working all day
Our children will need supervision,
So we'd best find some help straightaway.'

'Book an au pair,' said our neighbour,
'It's only a few quid a week.'
Au pair: another name for slave labour,
They only come here to learn how to speak.

So Gemma arrived from Belgium,
It's crazy how little we paid.
She was learning her English from toddlers,
But not very much I'm afraid.

Bottles soon became 'boccles';
She learned 'din dins', 'wee-wee' and 'poo'.
Then she asked at our railway station
What time's the next 'puff-puff' due?

This tale has a happy ending:
Gemma stayed on for a couple of years.
When she left we knew we'd all miss her –
There were smiles and a few little tears.

She now speaks better English than we do,
She's passed her exams in law.
She's a qualified tutor at Cambridge,
And she lectures on Radio Four.

Clichés

Some people try to talk highbrow,
With phrases they hope will amaze,
Proverbs and corny quotations,
And we live in a world of clichés.

'Every day' is now 'twenty-four/seven'
And 'you made the stage your own'.
We are always reminded 'the bottom line is . . .'
And that 'you'll never walk alone'.

Put your 'best foot forward',
And 'your shoulder to the wheel';
'Stand with your back to the wall'.
'Put your nose to the grindstone'
And 'march boldy on' . . .
If after that you can walk at all!

'Rome wasn't built in a day', they say,
And 'it's a yes from me',
You 'raised the bar', you 'nailed it',
And 'the best things in life are free'.

'It's a no-brainer', we're constantly told,
Are we 'in danger of losing the plot'?
Everyone's trotting out clichés
And the language is going to pot.

So 'step up to the plate' before it's too late,
All this silly talk is a pain.
'I've seen the light!', 'we have lift off!'
So let's just talk proper again.

Descriptive Words

We have words for single and plural,
Which we've used since English began,
Like a 'flock' of sheep and a 'gang' of crooks,
But inventing new words is my plan.

Try a 'bevvy' of alcoholics;
Or a 'screech' of mother-in-laws;
A 'Galaxy' of chocoholics;
And a new name for ''er indoors'.

Here's a few more descriptions:
A 'snatch' of muggers sounds right;
Or a 'snooze' of sleepy politicians;
And an 'absence' of waiters tonight.

A 'gaggle' of stand-up comedians;
A simple 'jam' of tarts;
An 'attitude' of teenagers;
A 'corporation' of men who play darts.

A 'number' of mathematicians;
A 'flood' of plumbers as well;
A 'cupful' of leggy starlets;
A 'scoop' of reporters who tell.

I could sit playing Scrabble for hours.
When it comes to words, I'm no stooge;
Using my literary powers
And finding big words like 'huge'.

Name Changes

We all know that time will never stand still
And fashions get rearranged
But I don't understand and I never will
Why the names for children have changed.

What happened to the ones we used to love
Like Nora, Maggie and Flo?
And where have all the Fannies gone?
No one seems to know.

Most old names have disappeared
And new ones have taken their place.
We no longer hear Ada or Mabel
But at least we're still saying Grace.

And Gertrude, that name had a certain charm.
What a shame it's no longer about.
Everyone used to call her Gert
And leave the 'rude' bit out.

There's no joy if you call your boy Wally.
He'll have a tough time at school.
They wouldn't show mercy if he was a Percy
And Cedric isn't too cool.

But what's wrong with Bill and Bert or Cyril,
Polly or Chloe or Nell?
Let the kids all choose their own name,
They have to like it as well.

Don't lumber them with crazy tags
Like Twinkle or Chardonnay.
Give 'em a name they'll be proud of.
They'll thank you for that one day.

When our neighbour calls to her young ones
We do our best to suppress our grins.
For when all's said and done, it can't be much fun
For Quasimodo and Adolph, her twins.

This woman's had fourteen children.
She called the last one Ritz.
She's not sure what to call the next one.
We think she should call it Quits.

13

Christmas Cheer

Christmas for many children means a trip to the theatre to watch a pantomime. I've acted in twenty-one pantomimes over the years and certain moments stand out. When I was playing Buttons in Cinderella, *I invited some children on to the stage to receive a present from my shopping trolley. I picked one dour-looking boy to talk to, thinking I'd cheer him up.*

'And what's your name?' I asked.

'Stephen,' he said.

'Stephen! Is that with a "ph" or a "v"?'

He stared at me. 'It's with an "S" you twit!'

Have you ever tried to analyse pantomimes? Kids love them but do they understand them? Americans certainly don't!

Pantomimes

I've got a friend who lives in New Jersey,
And over a glass of wine,
He said, 'What do you know about a kid's Christmas show,
Something called a "Pantomime"?'

Americans can't believe they're for children.
The plots are quite hard to convey.
'Some bits must puzzle the youngsters,' he said.
I'll admit they are a bit grey.

The principal boy is a woman!
The dame is a man in a dress!
Two men, of course, dress up as a horse,
And Dandini is anyone's guess.

There's a panto called *Jack and the Beanstalk,*
Where Jack swaps the cow for some beans.
It might be confusing, but kids find it amusing
Till the giant appears on the scene.

Pantos come in all shapes and sizes:
Some funny, some phoney, some twee.
Robin Hood, Mother Goose and *Aladdin,*
But *Cinderella*'s the best one for me.

Cinderella has two ugly sisters
(And again they're both played by men),
They don't like her at all but she goes to the ball
And gets into trouble again.

She nearly turns into a pumpkin,
But makes a hasty retreat,
Then the prince finds one of her slippers
And falls madly in love with her feet.

The slipper fits, and so they get married,
What joy, what fun, what a thrill.
You can learn a great deal at a panto:
Oh no, you won't! Oh yes, you will!

So this year, take the kids to a panto.
For a while, be a child in a game.
But it's easier to explain Esperanto
Than why the lead guy is a dame.

It's been fun writing Laughter Lines *and I have tried to include at least a little humour with each offering. But that is not the case with 'Yes, There is a Santa'. I originally wrote that as a song.*

Shirley Temple, the world famous young film star, was once asked in a television interview if she still believed in Father Christmas.

'Of course I do,' she said. 'But when I was six, my mother took me to a large store and introduced me to Father Christmas. He said, "Hello," then he asked me for my autograph!'

Yes, There Is A Santa

So they say there is no Father Christmas,
And they say there is no Santa Claus,
That reindeer can't fly – it's all a grown-up lie.
Well, maybe you and I should talk.

There's Peter Pan and Superman and
The Easter Bunny too.
They don't exist, say the pessimists,
But if you believe, then they do.

Miracles happen every day,
Things we can't visualize.
The greatest joys are the ones in our hearts
And not the ones before our eyes.

You can't see God but he's always there,
You can't touch love but it's real.
And dreams can come true in different ways,
Which only time can reveal.

So no more doubts and no more tears
And you will find through the years
If you believe each Christmas Eve
There will be a Santa, there'll always be a Santa.
Yes, there is a Santa Claus.

Hampson

The Turkey Has Landed

Every Christmas we used to have chicken,
It's something we've always been fed.
But this year I didn't want 'finger lickin''
So I bought us a turkey instead.

I laid the bird down by the oven.
I got a recipe book out as well.
I was determined to cook it correctly,
Like they would in a top-rate hotel.

First I removed all the feathers.
That's what the cookbook said.
I was plucking at feathers for hours,
But the next bit filled me with dread.

The recipe page said 'Paxo and sage –
It's important you stuff the thing right.'
Well, I stuffed for an hour, had a break and a shower,
Then carried on stuffing all night.

I filled the bird with the stuffing.
I found a packet of giblets too.
I wasn't sure what they were for,
So I stuck 'em on the fridge with some glue.

But the turkey didn't look right to me.
It was cold and clammy and white.
It had gone as limp as a lettuce,
Like it had been in a terrible fight.

I finally got the bird in the oven,
But the heat was too high I fear.
It went all dry and wrinkly
And some sparks came out of its rear.

It may sound like a joke, but it went up in smoke!
All the alarms went off (no surprise).
Then the firemen arrived but we'd all survived
So we gave them some tea and mince pies.

I'm happy to say we had lunch out next day,
With no word of that bird, I felt perky.
Well, what had occurred was simply absurd
And referred to as my 'murky turkey'.

The Sales

I am sitting here in A&E
Biting my fingernails.
I am not quite sure what happened to me,
But I went to the New Year sales.

It was like a stampede when they opened the doors,
Or the Charge of the Light Brigade.
Everyone heading for different floors
Like lunatics on parade.

There was pushing, gouging and tripping,
We became the walking wounded,
Some big woman turned me upside down
And asked, 'Are batteries included?'

And the cubicles where you try on things,
They really are too small.
It was like a rugby scrum in there
With people wall to wall.

I went in looking fine (or at least up to par)
In an old suit I'd bought at Burtons,
I came out wearing a push-up bra
And a pair of new lace curtains.

Yes, the bargains were unbelievable,
With offers you couldn't refuse.
But while I was trying on flip-flops
Someone bought my shoes.

I remember some big man then trod on my toes –
That's when the real quarrel started.
I got whacked in the mouth with his iPod
And two of my front teeth departed.

So here I am now in A&E,
Feeling a little bit rough.
Next year I won't bother with the New Year sales,
I think I've bought enough.

14

Helpful Advice

Very few things in life are quite as bad as we think they are and rarely, if ever, is anything as good as we imagine. So I've learned it's best to greet any minor disappointment with a friendly 'hello'. And if something appears to be going well for me, I try not to overreact. That doesn't mean we can't enjoy the good times – of course we should. And when the not-so-good times arrive, we should try to see them for what they are – a temporary blip.

I remember one evening being interviewed on a live television show. At times like that it's important to be relaxed and in control, but that particular night I was finding it difficult because as the red light went on, one of my eyelashes somehow managed to drop down across my line of vision. To me it looked and felt like a small log and I was convinced the viewers would be saying, 'What's wrong with his eye?' But I got through the show and to my amazement not one person had noticed what I had thought of as a drama.

I think that now and again we are all guilty of worrying too much about our appearance, but I doubt we are ever going to look quite as good or as bad as we think we do. So be nicer to yourself and stop worrying!

Incidentally, I think it was Les Dawson who said he was once met at a stage door only to be told, 'I hope you've got a good memory for faces because there's no mirror in your dressing room!'

HAMPSON

I Was Lying In My Bath

Something strange happened this morning.
I was lying in the bath, as you do,
I was happily counting my blessings
When a funny thought came through.

Why do things look bigger underwater?
My knees looked like frying pans,
My loofah resembled Gibraltar,
And my soap bar the Isle of Man.

Was it all a visual illusion?
A distortion of what we see?
I've come to a simple conclusion:
We only see what we want things to be.

I used to look in the mirror each morning,
I was happy with what I saw.
Then I started wearing contact lenses,
Now I don't look so good any more.

But being beautiful inside is what matters,
Of that I have no doubt.
And many of us could be beautiful,
If we could turn ourselves inside out.

Now you don't have to win the lottery
Or drive a big flashy car.
You don't have to be a celebrity,
You don't have to be a star.

Just keep telling yourself you're a winner.
Keep that thought in your heart and your soul.
You may make a mint but if you don't and you're skint,
You can just go and sign on the dole.

Be Inspired

Sometimes we take things for granted.
The radio, the TV, the phone.
And if there's a strike or a power cut,
Every man and his dog starts to moan.

We have miracles now at our fingertips,
Procedures that help us survive,
Incredible new discoveries which aid our recoveries,
Medicine that keeps us alive.

Inspiration arrives unexpectedly,
How or why no one can say.
The Dambusters idea from Barnes Wallis
Was born in a very strange way.

He was sat in his bath one morning,
With the soap-on-a-rope in his hand.
Then a brilliant idea began dawning
And the Dambuster bomb was planned.

We have computers today and the Internet,
Astronauts are fired into space.
Well, here's a plea now to every inventor,
A challenge you all can embrace.

Please be inspired: an invention's required.
Something every man's needing today –
Something quite cheap that we just have to bleep
And it keeps the wife's mother away.

Good Advice

We've all made mistakes along the way –
Boo-boos, faux pas and blips.
But as a graduate of life's university
I feel qualified to give a few tips.

Teamwork is definitely essential.
In fact, it's the name of the game.
Then if something you do goes belly up
Someone else can take the blame.

No, I don't think that I'm Mr Know-It-All,
And you don't have to do what I say,
But here's a few tips to consider,
A few thoughts that I'd like to convey.

One good turn gets most of the bedclothes.
There can be no flowers without rain.
Only borrow money from pessimists –
They don't expect to see it again.

Here's another tip to remember,
If you think no one cares about you:
Try missing a few mortgage payments,
And you'll soon find out they do.

Be sympathetic if someone's complaining,
Walk a mile in their shoes today.
And then when at last it stops raining,
You can just throw their shoes away.

If you lose something around the house
And you search from the roof to the basement,
The quickest way to find it again
Is to go out and buy a replacement.

Try not to drive at peak times,
Traffic jams are just never fun.
Here's the best way to beat the rush hour:
Make sure you leave work at one.

Do learn from all these friendly tips,
And keep this thought in your head:
If 'tomorrow never comes'
Don't worry about it: you're dead.

Well I hope my advice proves helpful
And it's lifted you up today,
But the men in white coats have now arrived
And they've come to take me away.

The Dentist

I'm supposed to go to the dentist today.
The mere thought of it fills me with dread.
That scary inspection, the dreaded injection;
I might go to the pictures instead.

Well that jab can make you sound silly.
Your gum goes numb and you spray.
Then the words come out willy-nilly,
In a sort of distorted way.

They sat one man in reception,
Not a word he said sounded clear.
The nurse – quite polite – asked, 'Are you all right?'
He said, 'Yesh, I'll just schit over here.'

Now I'm not a National Health patient,
I go 'private', where nothing is free.
I've found it's very expensive,
And the bill gets home before me.

One lady needed a tooth removed.
'How much will that be?' she enquired.
'Oh that'll be around a hundred pounds.'
That's when she nearly expired.

'A hundred pounds for a few minutes' work!
I'm not happy I want you to know.'
His reply was a bit sarcastic.
'Well if you want I can take it out slow.'

He cracks jokes while he's filling a cavity.
He tells folks he's putting in 'grout'.
He told one patient, 'Your teeth are fine,
But your gums have got to come out.'

Still I'll keep my date with the dentist today,
I'll just hope that the visit is brief.
'Cos I know what my friend Pam Ayres would say:
You should always take care of your teeth.

ACKNOWLEDGEMENTS

Writing this book has been a joyful and challenging experience and I would like to thank all who were involved in its publication, especially my literary agent Gordon Wise. Thank you, Gordon, for believing in these comedy verses from day one.

I send a big thank you to editor Ingrid Connell at Pan Macmillan. Hearing Ingrid giggling out loud every time I read her my next 'poem' was a genuine source of inspiration. And, of course, a big thank you to her team.

As ever, my PR agent Pat Lake-Smith has been more than helpful, especially with her instinct that I should contact Gordon Wise with these 'laughter lines'.

Finally, I send a special thank you to the Ellington family – that's Lance, Mirelle, Lauren and Lois. Their friendship and encouragement have helped in so many different ways.